THE RHETORIC COMPANION

A Student's Guide to Power in Persuasion

ANSWER KEY

THE RHETORIC

A Student's Guide to Power in Persuasion

COMPANION

⫷ ANSWER KEY ⫸

N. D. WILSON

DOUGLAS WILSON

canonpress
Moscow, Idaho

Published by Canon Press
P. O. Box 8729, Moscow, ID 83843
800–488–2034 | www.canonpress.com

N. D. Wilson and Douglas. Wilson, *A Rhetoric Companion:*
A Student's Guide to Power in Persuasion
Copyright © 2010 by N. D. Wilson and Douglas Wilson.

Unless noted otherwise, all Scripture references are taken from the Authorized Version.

Cover design by Rachel Hoffmann

Printed in the United States of America.

Library of Congress Cataloging-in-Publication Data
Wilson, Douglas.
 The Rhetoric Companion answer key / Douglas Wilson and N.D. Wilson.
   p. cm.
ISBN 978-1-59128-103-0
 1. English language--Rhetoric--Study and teaching. 2. Report writing--Study and teaching. 3. Academic writing--Study and teaching. I. Wilson, Nathan D. II. Title.
PE1404.W547 2011
808'.042--dc23
                    2011035204

11 12 13 14 15 16 17 18 19 20   9 8 7 6 5 4 3 2 1

Contents

Lesson 1   Biblical Wisdom and Rhetoric 9

Lesson 2   The Purposes of Rhetoric. 10

Lesson 3   Basic Copiousness 11

Lesson 4   Invention: The First of the Five Canons. 12

Lesson 5   Arrangement: The Second of the Five Canons 13

Lesson 6   Style: The Third of the Five Canons 15

Lesson 7   Memory: The Fourth of the Five Canons 16

Lesson 8   Delivery: The Fifth of the Five Canons 17

Lesson 9   Ethos 18

Lesson 10   Pathos. 20

Lesson 11   The Basics of Reasoning. 21

Lesson 12   The Structure of Argument 22

Lesson 13   Syllogisms: Categorical and Hypothetical 26

Lesson 14   Fallacies on the Street 1 28

Lesson 15   Fallacies on the Street 2 30

Lesson 16   Fallacies on the Street 3 31

Lesson 17   The Poetry of Argument. 32

Lesson 18   Invention, Stasis, and the Exordium. 34

Lesson 19   Invention, Stasis, and the Narratio. 36

Lesson 20   Invention, Stasis, and the Confirmatio and Refutatio 37

Lesson 21   Invention and Arrangement 38

Lesson 22   The Rhythm of Words 1 40

Lesson 23   The Rhythm of Words 2 43

Lesson 24   Still More Rhythm of Words 44

Lesson 25   Metaphor and Style 45

Lesson 26   Indirect Information 46

Lesson 27   Style and Reading 47

Lesson 28   Elocution 48

Lesson 29   Stance and Gestures 49

Lesson 30   Eye Contact 50

Lesson 31   Putting It All Together 51

LESSON 1 - Biblical Wisdom and Rhetoric

1. Where does the almost-universal suspicion of rhetoric come from?
   - The suspicion goes back at least to Socrates, because "rhetoric" has often become synonymous with "manipulative sophistry."

2. Is this a biblical suspicion?
   - The suspicion of rhetoric was first of all a pagan suspicion, although the Bible does reject a certain kind of rhetorical sophistry.

3. What is the position of rhetoric in the Trivium?
   - Rhetoric is a sort of halfway point between the Trivium and the Quadrivium.

4. What is the Quadrivium?
   - The Quadrivium is the last four of the seven liberal arts: arithmetic, geometry, astronomy, and music.

5. What is sophistry?
   - Sophistry is a manipulative system of tricks of logic and diction, with the goal of winning a case irrespective of the "right" side or the "right" way to win.

6. Does I Corinthians 1:17–2:13 require Christians to reject rhetoric? Why or why not?
   - No. Paul rejects rhetoric when it pretends to be autonomous and not under Christ and the Gospel: a Christian must speak honestly and plainly. But a Christian must also speak appealingly, thoughtfully, and deliberately, which is the subject of rhetoric.

LESSON 2 - The Purposes of Rhetoric

1. What is the definition of rhetoric we are using in this book? How does the Christian faith affect the definition?

- Quintilian's definition is that rhetoric is the art of a good man speaking well. However, all these terms must be defined biblically: rhetoric is the art of a godly man speaking well in his attempt to persuade others to believe and act in accordance with biblical wisdom.

2. What are the three purposes of rhetoric?

- Rhetoric is meant to deal with ignorance, bring about like-mindedness, and motivate to action.

3. What was Aristotle's definition of rhetoric? Are there any problems with it?

- Aristotle's definition of rhetoric: "The power of discovering the possible means of persuasion in reference to any subject whatever." This definition allows for means of persuasion not in the least bit oratorical, and is more appropriate for the process of invention.

4. What are the three kinds of rhetoric in the ancient classification?

- The three categories of ancient rhetoric are Judicial (guilt or innocence), Deliberative (courses of action), and Epideictic (praise or blame).

5. Have there been any developments in "kinds" since then?

- Christianity adds the categories of Preaching (proclaiming the word of God—what to believe) and Teaching (expounding the word of God—what to do).

LESSON 3 - Basic Copiousness

I. What is copiousness? Why is it important for your speaking?

• Copiousness refers to the material (phrases, experiences, knowledge, etc.) out of which a rhetor composes his oratory. If you are very copious, you will have taken in many things to draw from when you speak; whereas, if you know nothing except what you've learned from sitcoms, your speech will suffer.

2. What are the two definitions of "commonplace"?

• "Commonplaces" can either refer to 1) commonly held worldview phrases circulated in every community, or to 2) quotations, phrases, and poems to aid the flow of the speaker's copiousness and to influence the speaker's voice.

3. What retards copiousness?

• A slack lifestyle and overconsumption of popular entertainment.

4. What are some good ways to achieve copiousness?

• Read the Bible and good books. Read lots of books. Collect words by reading dictionaries and other word tools. Read aloud to yourself. Record and use great commonplaces.

5. What is the effect of copiousness on the listener?

• A copious speaker will always leave the audience wanting to hear more.

LESSON 4 - Invention: THE FIRST OF THE FIVE CANONS

1. **What are the five canons of rhetoric? Be prepared to define and discuss each of them.**
   - Invention: coming up with content (proofs).
   - Arrangement: clearly and persuasively organizing arguments.
   - Style: using good syntax and diction.
   - Memory: remembering the arguments.
   - Delivery: saying the arguments.

2. **What are the three kinds of proof? Under which canon of rhetoric are they to be studied?**
   - The three kinds of proof are ethos, pathos, and logos. They are studied under Invention, because all means of oratorical persuasion fall under one of these three kinds of proof.

3. **Explain why each is legitimately a species of proof.**
   - Because the questions "Who am I?," "Who are they?," and "Where am I trying to get them?" are always relevant, and every situation necessarily involves elements of ethical, pathetic, and logical proof.

4. **What is stasis theory?**
   - Stasis theory is a means of helping the speaker discover the fundamental point at issue.

5. **What is Invention?**
   - Before you can say anything, you have to "come up" with something to say. Coming up with the content is called invention.

LESSON 5 - Arrangement: THE SECOND OF THE FIVE CANONS

1. What is arrangement?
- Arrangement deals with clearly and persuasively organizing arguments.

2. What is the basic arrangement of a speech in classical rhetoric?
- The basic arrangement of an entire classical speech is: Introduction, statement of facts, proofs, and conclusion.

3. What is the detailed arrangement?
- The more detailed arrangement of an entire classical speech is: exordium, narratio, partitio, (propositio), confirmatio, refutatio, and peroratio.

4. What is an exordium?
- An exordium is an introduction or glimpse of what is to come, intended to hook the audience.

5. What is partitio?
- The partitio is the outline of the whole speech.

6. What is the propositio?
- The propositio is the thing the speaker is attempting to show: the point of the speech (the thesis statement).

7. What is the narratio?
- The narratio depicts the facts of the case and the material to be used later in the speech.

8. What is the refutatio?

- The refutatio anticipates and answers objections to the propositio.

9. What is the peroratio?

- The peroratio is the concluding remarks.

10. What is confirmatio?

- The confirmatio is the presentation of the arguments.

LESSON 6 - Style: THE THIRD OF THE FIVE CANONS

I. What is style?
- Style is the sum total of the aesthetics of your speech, based on correctness, clarity, language style, ornament, and sentence structure.

2. What are the three levels of style? Give an example of each.
- Grand: "Good evening."
- Middle: "Hello."
- Plain: "Hi."

3. What are the five elements of style?
- The five elements of style are: Correctness, clarity, language style, ornament, and sentence structure.

LESSON 7 - Memory THE FOURTH OF THE FIVE CANONS

I. **What is memory?**

- Memory is like a muscle - the more you use it, the more you will be able to do with it, and the stronger it becomes. It is the ability to fill your mind with many different things about the world, review the contents of your mind, and then use said things wherever appropriate.

2. **What is the memory device recommended in the** *Rhetorica Ad Herennium?*

- Connect things you want to remember to things with which you are already familiar.

LESSON 8 - Delivery: THE FIFTH OF THE FIVE CANONS

I. What is delivery?
- The fifth canon of rhetoric has to do with presenting the final product once it has been invented, arranged, ornamented and memorized. It encompasses both voice and gesture.

2. What is the Greek term for it?
- *Hypokrisis*: the work of an actor who responded to the chorus in a tragedy.

3. According to Aristotle, what are the three important elements of your vocal delivery?
- In delivery, Aristotle emphasized voice, pitch, and rhythm.

4. What is the other important aspect of delivery?
- Gesturing, whether with head, eyes, hands, etc., is an important aspect of delivery.

LESSON 9 - Ethos

I. **According to Quintilian, what are the four characteristics which are important for ethos?**

  - For Quintilian, the four characteristics of ethos are: Courtesy, kindliness, moderation, and benevolence.

2. **What is the difference between invented ethos and situated ethos?**

  - For invented ethos, a speaker can create his ethos for an audience which does not know him by means of stories, intonation, and other elements of delivery. With situated ethos, a speaker uses the reputation he already has before an audience which more or less knows him.

3. **Which one lends itself more readily to a situation where the speaker is coming from out of town and is new to the audience?**

  - A speaker from out of town will have to rely almost entirely on invented ethos.

4. **What is rhetorical distance?**

  - Rhetorical distance describes how close or far away an audience feels from the speaker.

5. **What does grammatical voice do to distance?**

  - Depending on skill and method, grammatical voice can be used to draw an audience close and identify with a speaker, or to keep the audience at a distance.

6. **What does formality do to distance?**

  - Formal speech keeps a speaker and audience separated (although inappropriate informality could distance an audience, as well).

7. **What does verb tense do to distance?**

  - Present tense is immediate and feels close and alive (i.e. in storytelling).

8. What do the active and passive voice do to it?

- The passive voice tends to create distance by removing responsibility and making a conversation abstract. The active voice, especially when combined with the 1st person, can often decrease distance.

9. What do qualifiers do to distance?

- Qualifiers decrease distance.

10. What do polysyllabic words do to distance?

- Polysyllabic words tend to establish an educated ethos, but they also increase distance.

LESSON 10 - Pathos

I. **What does it mean to prove something?**
- To "prove" something does not mean "to establish inerrant certainty" or "to convince." It is "to obligate belief"—to reveal something as true to your audience.

2. **What distinguishes a right use of pathos from simple manipulation?**
- The speaker must feel the emotion he is trying to evoke honestly, and the emotional proof must line up with the logos and pathos.

3. **What must we distinguish without separating?**
- We must distinguish (rather than separate) what we know cognitively and what we feel viscerally.

4. **What should the relationship between thought and tears be?**
- Thought cannot dominate tears, but tears cannot dominate thought, either. It's a balance.

5. **In what ways does the average age of the audience matter?**
- Younger audiences are generally more impetuous and emotional, whereas older audiences tend to be cynical. A speaker has to adjust the level of pathos depending on his audience.

LESSON 11 - The Basics of Reasoning

I. **What is the law of the excluded middle?**
- The law of the excluded middle: A statement is true, or it's false (nothing in between).

2. **What is the law of identity?**
- The law of identity: A true statement is true.

3. **What is the law of noncontradiction?**
- The law of noncontradiction: A statement cannot be true and false at the same time.

4. **What is a fallacy?**
- A fallacy is an argument that is somehow twisted with regard to what it is attempting or claiming to do.

5. **What is the difference between deductive and inductive arguments?**
- A deductive argument is logically valid or invalid—the premises necessarily do or do not imply the conclusion, no matter what terms there are. An inductive argument is strong or weak (they are all technically invalid, by definition). Deductive argument moves from general claims to particular. Inductive argument moves from particular claims to the general.

6. **What is a fallacy of form?**
- A fallacy of form occurs when the structure of an argument is wrong (the conclusion does not logically follow from the premises, no matter what they are).

7. **What is a fallacy of distraction?**
- A fallacy of distraction occurs when a response is intentionally used to change the subject while losing an argument.

LESSON 12 - The Structure of Argument

I. What is a statement?

- A statement is a sentence which can be said to be either true or false without contradiction.

2. What is a conclusion?

- A conclusion is what you are seeking to prove by means of the premises.

3. What is a premise?

- A premise is a reason for coming to a particular conclusion.

4. What is a fallacy?

- A fallacy is an argument that is somehow twisted with regard to what it is attempting or claiming to do.

5. What is a fallacy of form?

- A fallacy of form occurs when the structure of an argument is wrong (the conclusion does not logically follow from the premises, no matter what they are).

6. What is a fallacy of distraction?

- A fallacy of distraction occurs when something is used to distract from the central issues in the situation.

7. What is a deductive argument?

- A deductive argument is logically valid or invalid—the premises necessarily do or do not imply the conclusion, no matter what terms there are. Deductive arguments move from general claims to particular.

8. What is an inductive argument?

- An inductive argument is strong or weak, reasoning from particular to general claims.

9. What is a valid argument?

- In a valid argument, if the premises are true, then the conclusion is necessarily true.

10. What is an invalid argument?

- An invalid argument is an argument in which the conclusion does not necessarily follow from the premises.

11. What is a strong or weak argument?

- A strong argument is an inductive argument in which the general conclusion is pretty likely (since the particulars upon which the argument is based are of a reasonable size). In a weak argument, the specific particulars probably don't support the conclusion, or at least aren't enough to justify the conclusion by themselves.

12. What is the law of the excluded middle?

- The law of excluded middle: A statement is true, or it's false (nothing in between). There is no third way.

13. What is the law of identity?

- The law of identity: A true statement is true. Truth is truth.

14. What is the law of noncontradiction?

- The law of noncontradiction: A statement cannot be true and false at the same time. Truth excludes falsity.

15. What is the square of opposition?

- The square of opposition shows the relationships between all types of statements, and is a quick way to identify some problems within deductive arguments.

16. What is a universal affirmative?

- All S is P.

17. What is an A statement?

- An A statement is a universal affirmative statement.

18. What is a universal negative?

- No S is P.

19. What is an E statement?

- An E statement is a universal negative statement.

20. What is a particular affirmative?

- Some S is P.

21. What is an I statement?

- An I statement is a particular affirmative statement.

22. What is a particular negative?

- Some S is not P.

23. What is an O statement?

- An O statement is a particular negative statement.

24. What is a distributed term?

- A distributed term refers to a statement that is being made of every member of the class (every last S in "All S is P").

25. What is an undistributed term?

- An undistributed term refers to a statement that is being made of only some of the class (some of the P's in "All S is P").

26. What is a contrary relationship?

- If two statements have a contrary relationship, they cannot both be true but they can both be false.

27. What is a contradictory relationship?

- If two statements have a contrary relationship, they cannot both be true and they cannot both be false.

28. What is subcontrariety?

 • If two statements have a subcontrary relationship, they can both be true but they cannot both be false.

29. What is subimplication?

 • If a universal negative statement is true with specific terms, then the particular negative statement must also be true (implication of truth).

30. What is superimplication?

 • If a particular affirmative or particular negative statement is false, then the universal statement on the same side of the square must also be false (implication of falsity).

LESSON 13 - Syllogisms: CATEGORICAL AND HYPOTHETICAL

I. **What is a categorical syllogism?**
- A categorical syllogism is a kind of deductive argument consisting of three terms, two premises, and one conclusion.

2. **What is a major term?**
- A major term is the predicate of the conclusion.

3. **What is a middle term?**
- A middle term occurs in both premises but not in the conclusion.

4. **What is a minor term?**
- A minor term is the subject of the conclusion.

5. **What is a major premise?**
- A major premise is the premise with the major term in it.

6. **What is a minor premise?**
- A minor premise is the premise with the minor term in it.

7. **What is a sound argument?**
- A sound argument has a valid structure and is true.

8. **What is an unsound argument?**
- An unsound argument is flawed in some way. Usually, we use "unsound" to mean an argument that has a valide structure but a false premise.

9. **What is the mood of an argument?**
- A syllogism's mood is an abbreviation of the structure of the argument in terms of the square of opposition.

10. What is a figure in an argument?

- A syllogism's figure refers to the arrangement of the middle term in the argument.

11. What are the five rules of validity?

Five Rules of Validity:

- The middle term must be distributed in one premise.
- If a term is distributed in the conclusion, it must be distributed in its premise.
- A valid syllogism cannot have two negative premises.
- A valid syllogism cannot have a negative premise and an affirmative conclusion.
- A valid syllogism cannot have two affirmative premises and a negative conclusion.

12. What is the fallacy of affirming the consequent?

- Affirming the Consequent: An invalid syllogism of the form "If P, then Q. Q. Therefore P."

13. What is a fallacy of denying the antecedent?

- Denying the antecedent: An invalid syllogism of the form "If P, then Q. Not P. Therefore not Q."

14. What is *modus ponens?*

- Modus Ponens: A valid syllogism of the form "If P, then Q. P. Therefore Q."

15. What is a *modus tollens?*

- Modus Tollens: A valid syllogism of the form "If P, then Q. Not Q. Therefore not P."

LESSON 14 - Fallacies on the Street

1. What are fallacies of distraction?

- A fallacy of distraction occurs when the information that is offered in an argument is irrelevant to the conclusion presented.

2. What are fallacies of ambiguity?

- A fallacy of ambiguity occurs when the information that is offered in an argument is fuzzy or confusing.

3. What are fallacies of form?

- A fallacy of form occurs when the structure of an argument is wrong (the conclusion does not logically follow from the premises, no matter what they are).

4. What is the ipse dixit fallacy?

- *Ipse dixit* is an illegitimate appeal to authority.

5. What is the ad populum fallacy?

- *Ad populum* is an illegitimate appeal to the authority of a mass of people just because of their sheer numbers.

6. What is an ad baculum fallacy?

- *Ad baculum* is attempting to convince someone of an argument based on the negative consequences that would result from believing.

7. What is an ad hominem fallacy?

- *Ad hominem* is improperly attacking the person instead of the argument.

8. What is a Bulverism?

- A Bulverism is the assumption that an argument is wrong, followed by an attack of its proponent for the reason he believes it (when the person's reason for adopting the argument is not relevant to your argument).

9. **What is a tu quoque fallacy?**

- *Tu quoque* is pointing out an inconsistency in an opponent's behavior without defending an inconsistency in one's own behavior.

10. **What is an ad ignoratium fallacy?**

- *Ad ignorantium* is attempting to offer proof based on a lack of contrary evidence.

11. **What is chronological snobbery?**

- Chronological snobbery is rejecting a position simply because of how old or new it is.

LESSON 15 - Fallacies on the Street 2

I. **What is a fallacy of equivocation?**
- A fallacy of equivocation occurs when one of the terms in an argument has more than one meaning.

2. **What is a fallacy of accent?**
A fallacy of accent occurs when a sentence can have its meaning changed depending on where the emphasis is placed.

3. **What is a fallacy of selective arrangement?**
- A fallacy of selective arrangement occurs when a statement is made in such a way as to invite a false conclusion.

4. **What is the fallacy of amphiboly?**
- The fallacy of amphiboly occurs when an entire sentence, occurring as a whole, is ambiguous.

5. **What is fallacy of composition?**
- Fallacy of composition occurs when a speaker asserts that whatever is true of the parts must be true of the whole.

6. **What is the fallacy of division?**
- The fallacy of division occurs when a speaker asserts that whatever is true of the whole must be true of the parts.

LESSON 16 - Fallacies on the Street 3

I. **What is petitio principii?**

- *Petitio principii* is assuming what needs to proven, or begging the question.

2. **What is a post hoc ergo propter hoc?**

- *Post hoc [ergo propter hoc]* occurs when chronological priority is the only reason given for the assumed causal relationship.

3. **What is the either/or fallacy?**

- The either/or fallacy [bifurcation] occurs when a speaker presents a false dilemma and reduces multiple choices down to two options.

4. **What is a complex question?**

- A complex [loaded] question is a question that is asked in such a way as to exclude a legitimate response.

5. **What is apriorism?**

- Apriorism is a hasty generalization and inappropriate induction.

LESSON 17 - The Poetry of Argument

I. **What is the difference between expressions that are ordinary, scientific, and poetic?**
   - Ordinary expressions use straightforward words and phrases; scientific expressions tend to use quantitative and analytic expressions; and poetic expressions tend to use image and metaphor.

2. **Name three elements in the poetic approach to meaning.**
   - The poetic approach is imprecise because it uses qualification, concrete images, and oblique correlation.

3. **What is the difference between how we handle a poem and how we handle a mathematical table?**
   - We handle a mathematical table by looking for predictable regularities, logical arrangement, and strict definitions. We also want accuracy in a poem, but we test for it differently, looking at images and allowing feeling to have greater sway. In the end, it's much easier to be certain about mathematics than about a poetic interpretation.

4. **In the parable of the Good Samaritan, was the fellow who was beat up on the right side of the road or the left? Discuss.**
   - You walk on the left side of the road, and drive on the right. So the Samaritan was probably driving his donkey down the right side of the road, and looked to his left and saw the injured guy...

5. **What is a chiasm?**
   - A chiasm is a structural device whose beginning and ending points are related, and whose second and second-to-last points are related, and whose third and third-to-last points are related (etc.), with the most important elements coming in the center. (A, B, C, C', B', A')

6. How might this affect an outline?

- If a speech or story (i.e., many, many biblical passages) is structured as a chiasm, then we should perhaps think about outlining in a different way than a typical "one to ten" outline, because linear order is frankly less relevant.

LESSON 18 - INVENTION, STASIS, AND THE Exordium

I. What is stasis theory?
- Stasis theory is the process of determining the issue in the argument, or the point of disagreement.

2. Where does the word stasis come from?
- *Stasis* comes from a Greek word, meaning "stand."

3. What is the difference between a definite (or specific) and indefinite (or general) issue?
- A specific or definite issue deals with actual situations, persons, places, or events, whereas a general or indefinite issue involves situations that have a broad area of application.

4. What is hypothesis?
- Hypothesis is a specific or definite issue.

5. What is the thesis?
- Thesis is a general or indefinite issue.

6. Give an example of each.
- Hypothesis: Brutus should not have stabbed Julius Caesar. Thesis: It is immoral to assassinate a political leader.

7. What does Quintilian say about subdividing the general questions further?
- Quintilian says general questions can be subdivided into questions of knowledge and questions of action.

8. **What are the four staseis?**

   The four staseis are:
   - Conjecture: Does it exist?
   - Definition: What kind of thing is it?
   - Quality: Was it right or wrong?
   - Procedure: What should we do?

9. **What is the rhetor doing in the first stasis?**
   - In Conjecture, a rhetor is determining whether an issue even exists.

10. **The second?**
    - In Definition, a rhetor is determining what kind of thing or event is under discussion.

11. **The third?**
    - In Quality, a rhetor is determining whether an action was right or wrong, or whether we approve.

12. **Fourth?**
    - In Procedure, a rhetor is determining the proper course of action.

13. **Can a stasis ever be left out?**
    - Yes it's possible to not need to address one of the staseis in a discussion (although you will be able to find answers to all the staseis in most situations). As *The Rhetoric Companion* states: "It is better to pass by not only that which weakens the cause but also that which neither weakens nor helps it." For example, "What should we do about the Loch Ness monster?" (Procedure) is hardly relevant if the stasis we are discussing is, "Is there a Loch Ness monster?" (Conjecture). Or, on the other side, Conjecture ("Did it happen?") is not particularly useful when discussing, "Should the US have used nuclear weapons on Hiroshima and Nagasaki?" (Quality).

LESSON 19 - INVENTION, STASIS, AND THE Narratio

I. Is your narratio **part of your argument?**

- Yes, the narratio is part of the argument. It is where the speaker needs to layout everything necessary to build his case, and very little of what he doesn't need.

2. Where do you establish your definitions?

- You define long before you argue, but proper defining often determines the "winner."

3. What are some questions you might ask in conjecture?

- In Conjecture, you might ask: Does it exist? Is it true? Where did it start? What's the cause? Can it be altered or changed?

4. Definition?

- In Definition, you might ask: What kind of thing is it? What larger category contains this thing? What are its parts, and what are their relations?

5. Quality?

- In Quality, you might ask: Is this good or bad? Should it be avoided or sought out? Is this better or worse than the alternative? Is it more or less desirable than the available alternatives?

6. Procedure?

- In Procedure, you might ask: What should we/you/they do?

LESSON 20 - INVENTION, STASIS, AND THE

Confirmatio and Refutatio

1. **What is the simplest way to proceed in your invention for your refutatio?**
   - For the refutatio, look up some people on the opposite side of your stasis, see what their arguments are, and argue against those in your refutatio.

2. **What is a strategic point?**
   - A point is strategic if it meets two criteria: It is both decisive (the enemy's cause loses if you conquer here) and feasible (you actually *can* conquer here).

3. **What is an inescapable concept?**
   - An inescapable concept is one about which both sides must have an opinion: not whether there's moral imposition, but which morals will be imposed.

4. **How does this knowledge help you in preparing a talk?**
   - When you figure out inescapable concepts and strategic points, you can figure out and anticipate how to hit your adversary where it counts beforehand, and also make sure to limit the damage your adversary can do to your important arguments. In short, you can identify and fortify the hills you want to die on before the shooting and confusion starts.

LESSON 21 - Invention and Arrangement

I. **What did Quintilian say the exordium is for?**
  • Quintilian says the sole point of the exordium is to prepare the audience to listen to the rest of the speech.

2. **What should you guard against in the narratio?**
  • In the narratio, don't argue, don't be boring, and try to make the whole thing go down smoothly.

3. **What illustration did Quintilian use to describe the partitio?**
  • Quintilian says the partitio is establishing mile markers so the audience knows where they are in the speech.

4. **What should you do with a collection of weaker arguments?**
  • Use weaker arguments en masse so they can support one another.

5. **What should be avoided in the conclusion?**
  • In the conclusion, don't just summarize, and don't gloat.

6. **What are the two steps in arrangement?**
  • The first step in arrangement is picking which arguments you're going to use. The second step is placing them in an order that is clear and persuasive.

7. **What are the two types of exordia?**
  • The two kinds of exordia are introduction and insinuation.

8. **According to Cicero, what are the five types of situations which you might face?**
  • Cicero says you might have an honorable case, or it might be difficult, mean, ambiguous, or obscure.

9. **Give an example of each.**
   - Honorable: Discussing patriotism on Veteran's Day.
   - Difficult: Convincing your parents that you should smoke cigarettes.
   - Mean: Such-and-such-a-book is good literature.
   - Ambiguous: Hate crimes should be punished with suspension for school-aged children.
   - Obscure: The Giant Palouse Earthworm (*Driloleirus americanus*) should be listed as an endangered species.

10. **What did Quintilian say the narratio had to do?**
   - The narratio must state all the material of the case that will be used later on in a manner consistent with the facts we want believed.

11. **What do you do in the partitio?**
   - The speaker must point out important issues to be discussed by both himself and his adversary, and then he must outline the order in which his proofs will appear.

12. **What should the arrangement of your arguments be in your confirmatio? Why?**
   - Stronger, more independent arguments should come at the beginning or end of your confirmatio. Weaker arguments should be grouped together in the middle. That way the weaker arguments supplement each other, and the stronger arguments support all the weak arguments as a whole.

13. **What do you do in the peroratio?**
   - The conclusion should help support your logos, ethos, and pathos, by summing up arguments, attacking the ethos of the opponents, and awakening sympathy for the correct side.

LESSON 22 - The Rhythm of Words: I

1. What is poetry?

- Although establishing a precise definition is self-contradictory, poetry can be defined as "the metrical use of words and figures in imaginative and concentrated form."

2. What is meter?

- Meter is the pattern of stressed and unstressed syllables in words.

3. What is a foot?

- A metrical foot is two or three syllables.

4. What is an iamb?

- An iamb is a two syllable word, or two syllables in a row with the stress on the second syllable.

5. What is a trochee?

- A trochee is a two syllable word, or two syllables in a row in which the stress comes first.

6. What is an anapest?

- An anapest is a three syllable word, or three syllables in a row consisting of two unstressed syllables followed by a stressed syllable.

7. What is a dactyl?

- A dactyl is a three syllable word, or three syllables in a row consisting of a stressed syllable followed by two unstressed syllables.

8. What is tetrameter?

- Tetrameter is a line with four feet.

9. What is pentameter?

- Pentameter is a line with two feet.

10. Pick three of the quoted portions of poetry in this chapter, and discuss the meter exhibited in them.
    • Pg 109, Macbeth: trochaic tetrameter.
    • Pg 110, Dryden: dactylic tetrameter.
    • Pg 111, bottom: iambic tetrameter.

11. What is masculine rhyme? feminine?
    • Masculine: one syllable rhymes with another syllable.
    • Feminine: two syllables rhyme with another two syllables.

12. How is a rhyme scheme identified?
    • A rhyme scheme is usually identified by a notation of letters set off to the right of the poem.

13. How can meter be utilized in a prose oration? What is to be avoided?
    • You can use meter in prose to make important lines memorable and striking, and to generally beautify writing (c.f., Augustine).
    • Be sure to use it only in moderation, and not to be overly sentimental or painfully rhythmic.

14. Prepare five couplets of poetry of your own composing, using different meters. Present them, and afterwards be prepared to point out some of your metrical devices.
    • iambic pentameter:
    I'd like to wish upon a falling star / Except I'm old and cannot see that far.
    • trochaic trimeter:
    Mound the snow and whack it. / See the fissure? Pack it.
    • anapestic tetrameter:
    On a boat in the midst of the Caspian Sea / Lived a boy and a girl and a clam, happily.
    • trochaic dimeter:
    Question? Answer. / Singer? Dancer.
    • dactylic tetrameter:
    Once we admit that the Christ is our God, we'll stop / Killing our classmates, aborting our kids.

Some metric observations:

- Iambs produce a nice nursery-rhyme sound.
- Trochees sound like whacking and other forceful motions.
- Breaking the anapests at the end with a dactyl puts extra emphasis on "happily."
- Although —*ing* words are easy trochees (falling, singing, etc.), there are many other good trochaic words.
- Dactyls may not match the subject matter very well. Also, "stop" and "we" don't work too well as unstressed syllables.

LESSON 23 - The Rhythm of Words: 2

I. **What is poetry?**
- Poetry is concentrated writing with a meter that is identified and set apart (in distinction to prose).

2. **What is prose?**
- Prose is beautiful writing spread out, with a meter that meanders and hides.

3. **How can prose use iambs without being iambic?**
- Use short bursts of anapests, for example, to freshen up a mundane sentence. Don't use them until they get old—just sprinkle them here and abandon them there.

LESSON 24 - Still More Rhythm of Words

I. Give three examples of iambic words.
   iambic:
   • alone, because, destroy

2. Give three examples of trochaic words.
   trochaic:
   • brittle, naked, pithy

3. Give three examples of anapestic words.
   anapestic:
   • interrupt, understand, reelect

4. Give three examples of dactylic words.
   dactylic:
   • element, marvelous, liveried

5. Write a letter to the editor that you agree with (obviously), but your main point in doing it is to write a letter that has some metrical life to it.

   [Example]
   • I write on the errors of the dear Daily News...

LESSON 25 - Metaphor and Style

I. **What is style not to be considered as?**
- Style must not be an afterthought or something you try to deal with right at the very end of the composition process.

2. **In what way is the universe a figure of speech?**
- God created the entire world from his words. It's a divine composition.

3. **Why are all things cognates?**
- All things are cognates because they all, in some way, are revealing a facet of their Creator. This makes them all derivatives of the same root idea, the same "word family."

4. **How is this a foundation for metaphor?**
- In the Godhead, everything is like everything else—it is related in that it is created to give glory, and all things are declaring the majesty of one Word.

5. **If the Father speaks, and the Son is the spoken Word, then what is the correct interpretation?**
- The Holy Spirit is the divine hermeneutic.

LESSON 26 - Indirect Information

I. What is a motif?

- A motif is an image or a set of images which recurs in a number of instances and is meant to evoke, in an audience, certain expectations of things to come.

2. How does a motif communicate?

- Since a motif occurs often enough or in important enough contexts, a motif in a passage will immediately connote all the things usually connected with it. In this way, a motif brings its own context with it. This allows an author to adopt and mold a motif to his own purposes, using elements from it or leaving others out to highlight his own points.

3. What was ironic about Christ's use of the sign of Jonah?

- Jesus used the motif of Jonah in two ways—the obvious way is of course his death and resurrection. But just as appropriately, the sign of Jonah applies to Peter and the Pharisees, who fought and argued with the sending of God's son.

4. If someone demanded proof that a Western scene was preliminary to a gunfight, how could you provide that proof?

- You couldn't deductively prove that a Western scene necessitated a gunfight (and, of course, some authors deliberately misuse such motifs). But you could get to a pretty strong inductive argument for an imminent gunfight by bringing in a multitude of persuasive allies like John Wayne and Clint Eastwood (who, incidentally, would win the showdown).

LESSON 27 - Style and Reading

I. What is the importance of imitation in learning how to speak well?

• A man's reading and the company he keeps will shape his discourse. Good style doesn't happen naturally.

2. What did Quintilian set great importance on for this reason?

• Quintilian stressed the importance of those who raised children (in his time, a nurse or tutor; in ours, Mom).

3. Out of the quotations listed in this chapter, which was your favorite? Why?

[Example]

• I liked Bierce's definition of "exhort." He begins (as is his wont) with a positive word, and defines it so that widespread hypocrisy is neatly skewered. But he doesn't stop there: he adds a perfect simile to take his definition to a whole new level of perfection.

4. Which was your least favorite? Why?

[Example]

• Lewis' tree/train sentence exposes an interesting distinction, but it doesn't seem to be particularly beautiful or pithy after that. (Although now that I wrote that, "puffing" is the perfect word ever for a train verb-of-motion. I wonder if Lewis coined it.)

LESSON 28 - Elocution

I. **What is the quality of a person's voice?**
- Quality is the timbre or sound of a rhetor's voice.

2. **What does force mean?**
- Force is the variation of strength and weakness while speaking.

3. **What does pitch refer to?**
- Pitch is the highness or lowness of one's voice.

4. **What is the significance of movement in speaking?**
- Movement refers to whether or not a rhetor speaks quickly or slowly in general; of course, quickness and slowness can be used within a speech for specific emphasis.

5. **What is stress in speech?**
- Stress refers to which words are emphasized, but also to which *parts* of words are emphasized: beginning, end, vowels, consonants, etc.

6. **And what does interval refer to?**
- Interval refers to when a speaker pauses, and whether or not those pauses seem intentional.

LESSON 29 - Stance and Gestures

I. **Where should your feet be in the course of a talk?**
- Your feet should be shoulder width apart, one a little forward if you're a guy, and equal if you're a girl. They should stay that way for the whole speech, maybe moving once or twice.

2. **What is the importance of posture?**
- Good posture gives you more confidence and makes you more attractive to your audience. Posture also affects how you breathe, and as a result, how you sound.

3. **Why is lighting important?**
Lightning (or lack thereof) can prohibit you from seeing your notes, or can be a distraction if you're unfamiliar with your surroundings.

4. **What should gestures not do?**
- Gestures should underscore a point and not compete with it.

5. **What is the danger of affectation?**
- People notice gestures or words as affected if they drastically differ from the behavior you usually exhibit. People will call attention to it if it occurs, and they'll disrespect you for it. At the same time, honestly trying to improve your persona is not a danger.

LESSON 30 - Eye Contact

1. What two things should a speaker love?

- A speaker must love the material and the audience.

2. Is it bad to look down at a set of notes?

- If you are looking at the material because you're desperately trying to get familiar with it while presenting, that's bad.

3. What is the best way to establish eye contact with the group as a whole?

- Avoid looking at the back of the room, or the floor, or the ceiling. Move your eyes to where the people are and let natural forces do the rest.

4. What can looking at the material provide?

- Looking at the material can help with easing the transition between looking at one part of the audience and another.

5. What should the range of motion be for making eye contact?

- Generally, don't look more than 45 degrees to the right or the left.

LESSON 31 - Putting It All Together

I. In what sense is the universe a figure of speech? And in what sense is it not?

- The whole universe speaks about the glory of God—but obviously, it is not a perfect representation of divinity. That's where the metaphor part comes in.

2. How is the Logos important to this question?

- The whole universe was created from God's speaking and is sustained right now through the action of his Word

3. How does the created order speak about God?

- The created order speaks about God in metaphor: it declares his power and love and splendor and variety by showing the power and love and splendor and variety he built into it.

4. Why are all things "cognates"?

- All things are cognates because they all, in some way, are revealing a facet of their Creator. This makes them all derivatives of the same root idea, the same Word.

5. What makes effective metaphor possible?

- Effective metaphor is possible because God really did design similarities in creation, so saying X is like Z really is a true relationship, as long as X and Z relate in the way God made the world.

6. Why is the poet a "seer" more than a maker?

- The poet is not imposing his view of a certain thing upon the world: there is meaning and truth and poetry in things. Therefore, a poet is simply observing relationships that are really there, or being a seer.

7. Can anything therefore be a metaphor for anything else?

- No, a postmodern view of total relativity is not correct: a metaphor must actually get at the objective truth God created.

8. How should the discipline of seeing metaphor begin?

- To train yourself to observe metaphor, immerse yourself in the metaphors and figures of the Bible, the natural world, history, allusions, and literature (in other words, everything good).

9. How is the hypostatic union important to metaphor?

- Man is a fallen namer, and thus Christ becoming a human saves not only man's soul, but also his words, and naming in general. Jesus' man-ness means that even oratory is redeemed.

10. How does one's hermeneutic relate to the question of learning to speak with metaphorical richness?

- If a man is not aware of Christian history, there's no way he can see an accurate metaphor, because objects accept meaning (and thus similarities) only in their proper context. Words and stories have fuller meaning within the context of the proper worldview.

11. Give an example of a motif. How about a scriptural motif?

- A common motif is a man wearing a fedora in a small office, with his feet up on the desk, drinking from a flask: according to film noir, a blonde "dame" should enter the private detective's office at any moment. A scriptural motif is a barren woman: they always are given a child.

12. What does it mean to learn metaphor by imitation?

- Learning metaphor by imitation means that you must be so immersed and familiar with common metaphors that they ooze out of your pores every time you write or speak. The more you are around something, the more you will sound like it.

13. How can you profit through imitation?

- You can only profit from having your reading and company shape your discourse if you read and keep company with whom you would want to sound like. You must imitate good things.

14. **What is elocution?**
    - Elocution is the art of speaking distinctly, clearly, and well with regard to the pronunciation and relations of your words.

15. **What are the elements of elocution?**
    - The elements of elocution are: Quality, force, pitch, movement, stress, and interval.

16. **Be prepared to define each.**
    - Quality is the timbre or sound of a rhetor's voice. Force is the variation of strength and weakness while speaking. Pitch is the highness or lowness of one's voice. Movement refers to whether or not a rhetor speaks quickly or slowly. Stress refers to which words are emphasized, but also to which parts of words are emphasized. Interval refers to when a speaker pauses, and whether or not those pauses seem intentional.

17. **What is the relationship of musical instruments and public speaking?**
    - We can compare people's voices and speaking styles to musical instruments. Looking at where a specific instrument excels can often help determine what a speaker with a similar voice can do well.

18. **How should you begin to discipline your gestures?**
    - To begin disciplining gestures, catalogue the movements which are already natural and decide which ones you want to exclude to avoid distraction. Let someone who knows you help catalogue.

19. **What is the danger of affectation?**
    - When you attempt to adopt a style that is markedly different from the things you did before, it can often come across at least as strange, and at worst pretentious.

20. **What is the role of love in public speaking?**
    - A speaker must love the audience, and he must love the material. Loving those two things is a giant step toward obligating belief.

21. What are some of the mechanics of eye contact?

- For the mechanics of eye contact, look at the audience—not necessarily any specific members of the audience. Certainly don't watch the ceiling or the back wall. Try not to look more than 45 degrees to the right or the left. Look at your material if you need a break from the stares of the listeners.

22. What is confidence?

- Confidence is a matter of faith. If a speaker has faith in himself, his swagger will be obvious and off-putting to all (e.g. most rappers). If he has faith in God, he will be at ease, because love for the material and audience will fill him with a desire to bring the two together.

23. Be prepared to discuss the relations (again) of logos, ethos, and pathos.

- Logos, ethos, and pathos are always relevant in a speaking situation, and the nuances are something to carefully consider in specific cases. Since the Enlightenment, we especially must consider the importance of emotional and character proofs, because we tend to overemphasize logical argument.

24. What is the danger for speakers who are naturally gifted?

- Speakers who are naturally gifted are tempted to slack on practice and preparation, because they can still get a positive reception.

25. What is the danger for speakers who are not?

- It's easy for a speaker who is not gifted to give up. But it's important to remember that improvement (especially stylistic improvement) is always possible. Moreover, an individual will need to be an effective communicator, whether or not he's a naturally gifted public speaker.

CPSIA information can be obtained at www.ICGtesting.com
Printed in the USA
BVOW05s1059070913

330541BV00003B/55/P